AMBIGUITY

Aanavi chawla

First Published in April 2023

ISBN: 978-93-5741-330-5

E-ISBN: 978-93-5741-328-2

BLUEROSE PUBLISHERS

www.bluerosepublishers.com

info@bluerosepublishers.com

+91 8882 898 898

Cover Design:

Yash

Typographic Design:

Tanya Raj Upadhyay

Distributed by: BlueRose, Amazon, Flipkart

To everyone who supported me throughout; especially, Mrs. Babita Toshniwal and Mum, this one's possible only because of you!

Ambiguity

Am.buh.gyoo.uh.tee (noun)

A mixture of feelings or ideas that makes something hard to understand/confusing.

Synonyms: uncertainty; dubiety; etc.

Example : "Based on the at hand information, my theory is that every teenager's mind can be defined with one word, i.e., AMBIGUITY."

Angoraphobia >

FEAR OF LEAVING A 'COMFORT PLACE'
CLINGING ON TO THE PAST; FEARING CHANGE.

Enough, okay?
I know you don't wanna feel this way!

But that's what you gotta do;

Right now, you have to choose you.

Stop, okay?

Stop wondering how things could have been,

They turned out exactly how they were destined!

No matter how hard you try,

You can't mess with universe's decision,

Just wear your big girl pants and go through this transition!

It's okay to be sacred;

But you can't keep holding on instead!

What's done is done;

What's 'meant to be' is soon to come.

Atychiphobia>

FEAR OF FAILURE. GIVING UP/FLEEING DUE TO SMALL PROBLEMS.

This ocean won't ever become still, will it?
The ripples will only grow greater and greater,
The boats entering will only convince me to quit,
They'll manipulate me to just pass the equator.

But should I?
Should I accept this as my end?
Should I not try and pretend?
Should I not reach my happy end?

How will I?
How will I, if I keep letting these tiny things get to my
mind?
How will I, if I keep on waiting for the world to get a
lil kind!

Should I just give up?
Should I just flee?
No, how about I try something new: GET UP;
And think of ways to swim through this sea,
To swim through this sea!

Latibule>

A SAFE HIDING PLACE/ PERSON THAT BRINGS
YOU COMFORT.

YOU'RE THAT PERSON; NO ONE ELSE!

Powdering my flaws,

Hiding my scars,

Every day I wake up, to put on a mask:

A mask that shows abundant confidence,

A mask that makes me seem cold and mean,

What pleasure does deceiving the world give, you ask?

You only tell me, showing a weak person in front of traitors, is that a wise task?

You only tell me, is unmasking even a wise choice?

When everyone around is just waiting for you to devoice;

Crushing you is the only aim-

Those who say they care have something to explain.

The sooner you realise you it; the better,

Searching your soulmate when you've already met her?

You're the person who's in this forever,

So why wait for someone when you're no lesser?

Rumination>

CONTINUOUSLY THINKING ABOUT CERTAIN
THINGS THAT ROUSE SELF DOUBT IN MIND.

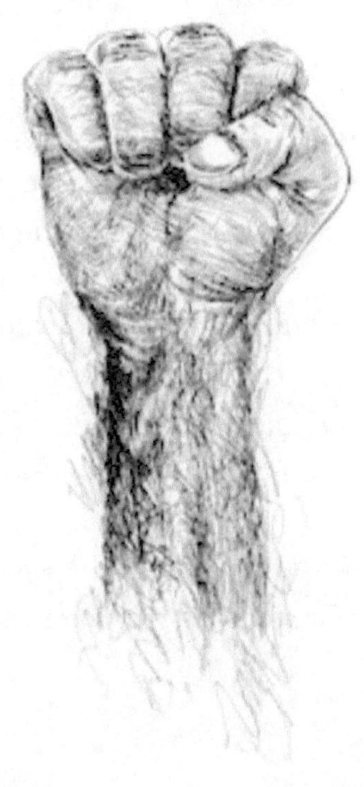

The next time when your body dysmorphia hits,
The next time your self-doubt suddenly clicks in,
The next time your overthinking shreds you to bits,
And the next time you feel clueless as to where to begin;
Remember:
Girl, you're a work of mastery just the way you are,
How dare you think that you're not a star?
How dare you think that you're a Bain?
This universe works for you darling,
Here, you're the character that's the MAIN!
You're incharge of your script here,
You decide who to keep near!
So the next time when you cast even a slightest bit of doubt at yourself,
I hope you hear my words "HOW DARE THOU" repeating to thyself!

Sciamachy>

AN ACT OF FIGHTING IMAGINARY EVILS; YOUR
DARK IMAGININGS.

I was lost inside my mind,
When the reality became hostile:
It shattered all the peace in mind,
Everything seemed undefined,
Nothing felt even a lil kind.
Flashbacks began to follow just like wind,
Everything perceived to be sinned-
The thread of life started to thin,
Memories commenced to masticate from within.
Time began to beat the clock,
Everything hurt as hard as a rock,
No one felt worthy enough to talk:
And the thoughts in the mind were stuck in the walk!

THINKING ABOUT THE SAME THOUGHTS IN A LOOP.

To think too much is a disease,
Once you cross that thin line; nothing seems to
appease,
Even a small mis-thought seems to tweeze,
The mind further makes the reprise,
Nothing anymore appears to please.
You start to fell caught:
Not by someone but your own thought;
Everything around tends to be a lot,
Intellect appears distraught-
Even to do a little thing seems like a CANNOT.

Rumination X Latiblue>

LATIBULE- SAFE HIDING PLACE ALSO CALLED FOXHOLE.

RUMINATION- OVERTHINKING.

RUMINATION CAN TURN YOUR HOME TO YOUR ENEMY BECAUSE OF THE NON EXISTENT SCENARIOS YOU MAKE WHILE RUMINATING.

I feel like I'm forever gonna be stuck in this foxhole,
Hiding away from all my trolls,
Thinking about things out of my control,
Hosting a bunch of polls:
Where is this foxhole?

I never seem to leave it behind,
When things get out of hand, it starts to rain;
But never so heavily that it uncovers my
confinement,
O dear, it's my BRAIN!

I thought foxhole was supposed to be safe,
My home has now become my enemy,
My hiding place has become unsafe-
What do I do Jeremy?

How do I stop from thinking so much?
How do I stop from replaying every little touch?
Can I just remove this tiny psyche of mine?
Maybe then I can draw the line....
Between my thoughts and the reality of this divine!

Pistanthrophobia>

FEAR OF TRUSTING PEOPLE.

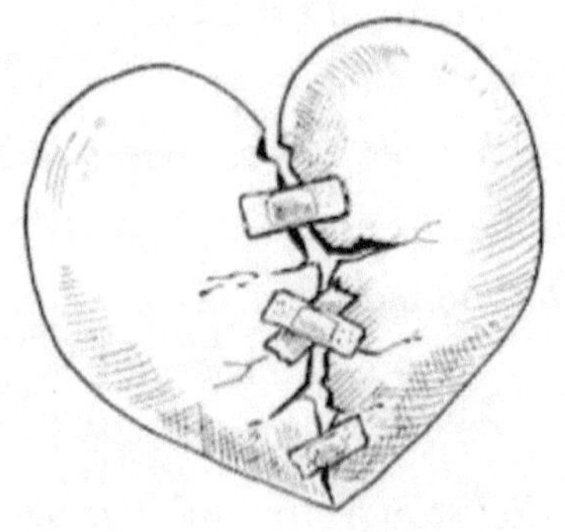

Trust no one,

Do you really think they care?

Just as soon as they are done,

They'll leave you with a tear.

Those promises and memories would start to seem voiceless,

The broken heart would definitely feel helpless,

That wonderful listener would no longer clear your mess,

And with this; you would've lost your benefactress!

Rumination>

Let your mind breathe:
Command your thoughts not to rush,
Don't think at all, just keep your thoughts hush;
Life's too beautiful to spend it in your mind,
Don't be so harsh on yourself, be a little kind?
You have this miraculous gift to be human;
You really want to waste it in this confusion?
Let's take it day by day;
Let's not think about tomorrow and make sense of today,
Let's enjoy the chirp of the morning bird,
Let's not be afraid to be a nerd,
Do/be whatever makes you happy;
Quit thinking about people, don't give them power to make your life crappy!

Anagapesis>

LOSS OF FEELINGS FOR SOMEONE YOU
FORMERLY LOVED.

Sometimes I wonder:
Why did you hurt me?
Do you even count it as a blunder?
Or just a mere mistake past this sea!
Did our ending hurt you too?
Or was it something you felt relieved for?
Sometimes I still question:
Whether were we something true?
Did you ever really love me or just screw!
Did you even consider me your shore?
Well, it doesn't even matter anymore;
There's nothing left to restore,
Nothing matters anymore!

I never thought I'd see this day so early,
I never thought I'd be left feeling so unworthy,
This maybe just a mere hurdle in life's journey,
But why does it feel like it will always hurt me.

I started to forget all my fears and give myself all in,
But boy, did I know I was building my heart a coffin?
Why did I stop recalling?
Recalling all the initial hurt; recalling all the fears I had,
Why did I think that maybe this time it won't hurt so bad?
Why did I think that maybe this time it won't even end first hand!

Being this blindfolded person never ended well in the past,
I thought maybe that suffering had surpassed,
Blinded by everything I didn't realise, the same thing was being recast;
The same thing was being recast.

Eleutheromania>

INTENSE DESIRE OF FREEDOM, OVER HERE
FROM SOCIETAL STANDARDS. EVERY BODY
TYPE IS UNIQUE AND BEAUTIFUL.

Looking at the mirror,
Seeing myself:
I can't express how much I hate myself,
Looking at her, even clearer,
Makes me even wanna consider hurting her for all those deserts,
I hate her for ruining all my efforts.
I am just aching to be accepted,
I just wanna be selected!
I am done being judged for the size of my thighs,
I just wanna be seen for my highs!
I am done being glared upon for having a wide hip,
I desperately wanna take that trip!
No matter how my body looks, I'm always gonna be ME,
When will this society finally agree?
When will I be accepted?
When will I be selected?

Rumination>

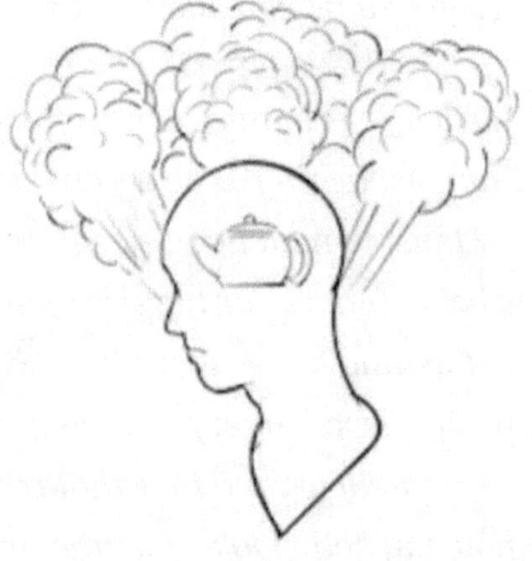

Can you stop frying your brain?

How long do you want to make your thoughts rain?

Calm this storm, stop making it thunder;

How much longer do you want to captivate her?

Deprive her from a normal life,

Confine her like an Afghan wife?

Does she no deserve to be carefree?

Does she not deserve to be unbound by the force of your decree?

Stop throwing non- existent problems at her,

There's nothing in this world she cannot conquer,

Just leave her alone for once and stop with these dark imaginings,

You'll see her shine with a light that's immensely dazzling!

I feel like I'm an outsider,
Trying to hold on a little bit tighter;
Annoying everyone around the moment I open my mouth,
Things for me always go south!
Why was I brought to this world?
I just feel like I'm twirled,
I feel like I'm the darkness,
Taking away all 'my people's' brightness!
Making the crowd dull,
For how long am I gonna be this numbskull?
Sometimes I wonder, "am I just caught?"
In this web of my mind, with a useless thought!
But then I conclude with finding me as the problem,
Why do I always have to stay so solemn?

Anagapesis>

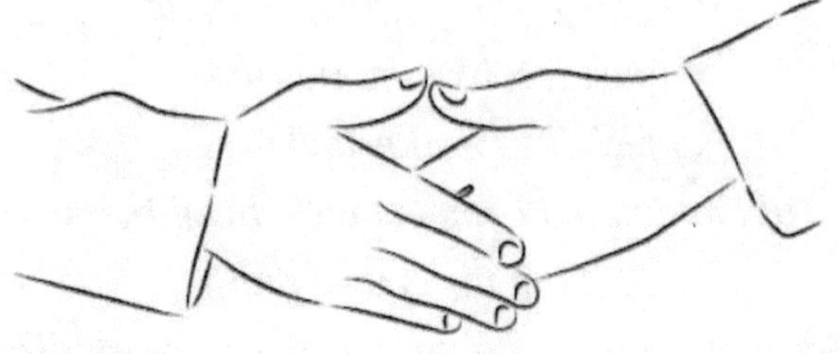

It's so hard to let go,
It feels like it's the end of the show!
Although it might be long ago,
What impairs most is the flashbacks you undergo,
They make you soo weak to and fro,
That every chance of letting go blows!

If you aren't going all the way;
Why stay till the midway?
Why not simply walk away?
Why stay till the midway?

Why not just leave today?
Why spend those valentine days?
Why even care today?
When you aren't going all the way!

Pistanthrophobia>

IT'S SOMETIMES OKAY TO ASK FOR HELP, LET YOUR GUARD DOWN, LET YOUR <u>FEAR OF TRUSTING OTHERS</u> FADE.

It's okay to ask for help, you know?
You can share with people what flows!
You don't have to keep rowing this boat alone,
Stop being so hard as a stone;
It won't make you look weak to be known,
It won't make you look strong to be on your own!
For god sakes; just reach out for once,
It won't make you look like a dunce,
Trust me, I get it;
I know you don't see this fit:
Sharing your problems with people-
Like it's something illegal!
Keep your ego aside and you'll know,
If you don't ask for help now, one day you'll overflow!

I lost today,
I lost today a battle which I thought I could easily win,
I thought things were going my way,
But overconfidence was bouncing off my skin.

I thought I was very well prepared,
This overconfidence poisoned my prep from within;
It became the major reason for my fall,
I'm devastated because I really thought I would stand tall.

Hey.

How've you been?

Don't tell me you're okay

How long do you wanna keep it all in?

It's not at all fine to keep it out of display!

It's not fine to let it eat you from within.

Don't feel that your problems are a burden!

You deserve an "I'm here person";

You should not let your dark imaginings think of you as any less

Because you my darling are not at all a stress.

I know you think that you are too much,

And you even think it's probably best if you keep hush,

But why do you want to conquer it all alone,

Why don't you get it, I don't want to keep even a single flaw of you unknown;

I wanna know it all:

And be there to pick you whenever you fall!

A part of me will always wonder why only I was blamed?

When everything was two-sided it was just I who you tamed?

Ignoring me to my face;

You could have just said you needed your space.

I don't want to strangle you in this friendship without your will,

But just so you know, I really love you still.

Anagapesis>

LOSS OF FEELINGS FOR SOMEONE YOU FORMERLY LOVED. UNCLOGGING OF YOUR VISION AS TO HOW THEY REALLY ARE.

I hope that you're super ashamed,
The way you treated me was just so astonishing;
But it was I, who you blamed?
For how long should I have tolerated you
demolishing me?
For how long should I have seen you crush me?
Believing your empty promises was my mistake,
What was not a mistake was setting myself free,
How many 'no talking' breaks should I take?
Cut off was an arrangement we should have made,
With every month we avoided it, made my hate grow
for you,
For treating me like something you never valued.

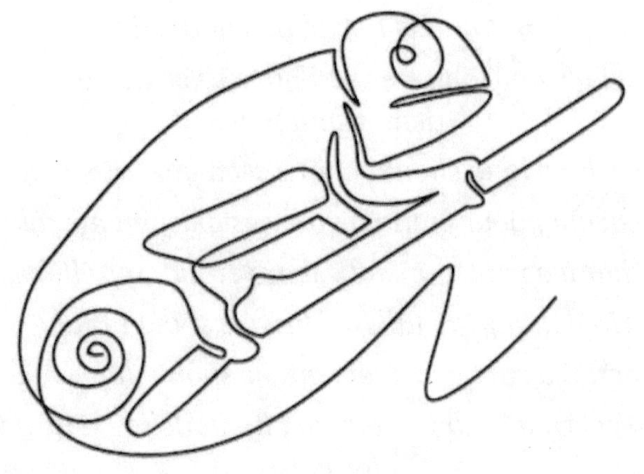

I trusted you;

I trusted you to be my home,

I counted you;

I counted you among the very few,

I showed you;

I showed you parts of me which no one knew,

I told you;

I told you the stories which were always unknown:

But you?

*You showed me what it was like to have a friend
similar to a chameleon,*

Your moves were really Machiavellian,

I blame myself for letting my guard down,

*When at the first deception I should have simply
turned around!*

Anagapesis >

People change, they say;
But do their habits change?
Does their toxicity pass away?
Or is it mask, for the world, they arrange?

Does their manipulative trait evaporate?
Do their words suddenly become legit?
Or is the reality initially kept separate?
Until they lose control and express it.

I'll ask you one question,
Are they worth your patience?
Is their love even true?
Or are they fooling you according to their
convenience?

Trust me, they're not worth it,
Choose yourself now and you'll be proud of it,
The attachment does not outweigh the emotional
abuse,
Be sensible and put a full stop to being used.

Self-Love>

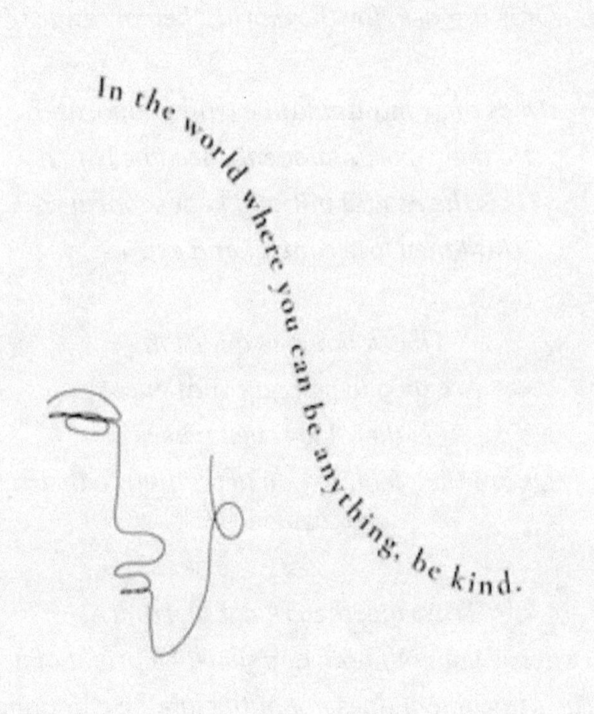

Love cannot be defined in words, isn't it?
Love is the most beautiful feeling until you quit.

Some say love is fire,
The fire which each soul requires.

Some say love is a clash of two lightnings,
Whose every sight for you can be very brightening!

Loving is not necessarily found in another soul,
Loving yourself is enough for your whole.

Loving yourself lightens you in every way,
Accepting yourself is the best gift you can give oneself each day!

Tackling with your flaws can be very arduous,
But trust me, running away from 'em can be extremely torturous!

From today; always remember, love comes from within,
Torturing yourself is no less than a deadly sin!

Lack of communication made us apart,
Creation of misunderstandings did all the imaginary
part,
Mind ached for another fresh start,
But it was the heart that wasn't smart..
And though the separation was a pain in the heart,
Both lived within one another like they've never been
apart.

Pistanthrophobia>

Trust is like a weapon,
Which is more than enough to make anyone threatened,
It gives no chance to the second,
And itself;
Is the biggest lesson!
Once broken makes a CONFESSION,
Of no longer dependence but only AGGRESSION!

The drop of tear from those beautiful eyes
Accompanied mournful cries,
Which said the final GOODBYE!
No space to speechify
Made a really hard tongue-tie,
After which the face had set drop dry!
When no one was left with any clue,
They broke time out of the true,
They had no time to screw;
She was in her own world, while he was broken
through!

It was this usual day;

I had a strange feeling since I left my bed;

I kept on assuring myself that everything was okay,

I kept on repeating to myself that it was all in my head,

I kept on telling myself that you'll always stay,

But guess what?

That same day you acted strangely,

Every inch of me started telling me to trust my gut,

Why was today the day when you had to behave so vaguely?

Maybe somewhere I knew you were looking for someone better;

Maybe today my gut was alarming me that you've now met her;

Maybe it was informing me that I was no longer needed,

Because if we're being honest; we both know I was someone you briefly heeded.

Why Ambiguity?

As mentioned at the very start, the meaning of "ambiguity" is 'uncertainty'. Relating that to my life, there have been so many mixed emotions throughout as I wrote this chapbook. Thus, deciding a single genre for the 'n' number of emotions seemed impossible. This title was 'the one' as in one word it defined my mind. As teenagers, aren't we all uncertain about numerous things? This chapbook is my uncertainty through my teen years; this has poems in which I've ranted about

the issues I faced: body dysmorphia, trust issues, overthinking, the feeling of being stuck in life, feeling emotionally drained, burnt out. This book rose in my notes app and I feel really grateful to have given it a hard copy form.

Life will keep throwing hardships at us, but it is our choice whether we give up or Keep our heads high through them till we reach 'our shore'. Life is a beautiful, complex, scary, overwhelming thing to get by: one might say life is very ambiguous. Let us help one another through this AMBIGUITY!

THE END.

9 789357 413305